Habitat Days and Nights

DAY AND NIGHT IN THE
Forest

by Ellen Labrecque

PEBBLE
a capstone imprint

Published by Pebble, an imprint of Capstone.
1710 Roe Crest Drive, North Mankato, Minnesota 56003
capstonepub.com

Library of Congress Cataloging-in-Publication Data
Names: Labrecque, Ellen, author.
Title: Day and night in the forest / by Ellen Labrecque.
Description: North Mankato, Minnesota : Pebble, [2022] | Series: Habitat days and nights | Includes
bibliographical references and index. | Audience: Ages 5-8 | Audience: Grades K-1 |
Summary: "Spend a day and night in the forest! Learn about this wooded habitat through the
fascinating animals that call it home. Leap from tree to tree with a squirrel searching for breakfast.
Pounce with a fox on the forest floor. Soar with a red-tailed hawk as the sun sets. After dark, build a
dam with a beaver. What will tomorrow bring in the forest?"-- Provided by publisher.
Identifiers: LCCN 2021041498 (print) | LCCN 2021041499 (ebook) |
 ISBN 9781663976932 (hardcover) | ISBN 9781666325393 (paperback) |
 ISBN 9781666325409 (pdf) | ISBN 9781666325423 (kindle edition)
Subjects: LCSH: Forest animals--Behavior--Juvenile literature. | Habitat (Ecology)--Juvenile
literature.
Classification: LCC QL112 .L328 2022 (print) | LCC QL112 (ebook) | DDC 591.73--dc23
LC record available at https://lccn.loc.gov/2021041498
LC ebook record available at https://lccn.loc.gov/2021041499

Image Credits
Flickr: MostlyDross, 16; iStockphoto: AVTG, Cover (forest), 1, lightstalker, Cover (bear), 1; Mighty
Media, Inc.: 20, 21; Shutterstock: BBA Photography, 7, Cynthia Kidwell, 9, Daniel Rodriguez
Garriga, 15, Danita Delimont, 17, G Allen Penton, 19, IgorCheri, 14, Inga Nielsen, 5, Jerry Morse,
13, Karen Hogan, 11, Matt Jeppson, 10, Photo_Time, 18, Ryan M. Bolton, 8, Tom Meaker, 6

Editorial Credits
Jessica Rusick, editor, media researcher; Kelly Doudna, designer, production specialist

All internet sites appearing in back matter were available and accurate when this book was sent
to press.

Table of Contents

Words in **bold** are in the glossary.

What Is a Forest?

A forest is a **habitat** filled with trees. Some trees have big, flat leaves. Other trees have leaves that look like needles.

Some forests are found in North America. They are home to many animals. Some animals come out during the day. Others come out at night.

A forest in North America

Morning

The sun rises over a North American forest. A gray squirrel hops from branch to branch. It has a big, bushy tail. The tail helps the squirrel stay balanced.

The squirrel collects nuts and seeds. It buries some of them underground. The squirrel will dig up this food in winter!

A squirrel burying food

Noon

A wood turtle crawls along a river. The turtle stamps its feet on the ground. This makes earthworms come out of the dirt. The turtle eats them!

Wood turtle

Black bear

A black bear climbs a tree. It uses its curved claws to grip the bark. The bear naps on a tree branch. It rests in the shade to avoid the sun.

Late Afternoon

A rough green snake lies on a tree branch. It warms its body in the sun. Then, the snake looks for a meal. It eats grasshoppers, crickets, and caterpillars.

Rough green snake

Great blue heron

A great blue heron stands in the river.
A fish swims by. The heron dips its head
in the water. It catches the fish in its beak.

Evening

The air cools as the sun sets. A mother cottontail rabbit checks on her nest. The rabbit's babies, or kits, are inside. The rabbit feeds her kits milk. Then she leaves.

The rabbit mostly stays away from her nest. This is so **predators** do not come near. The rabbit's kits are well hidden. She will check on them again tomorrow.

A cottontail rabbit kit in its nest

Night

A little brown bat searches for bugs to eat. The bat makes a high-pitched sound. The sound bounces off a moth. The bat uses this **echo** to find the moth.

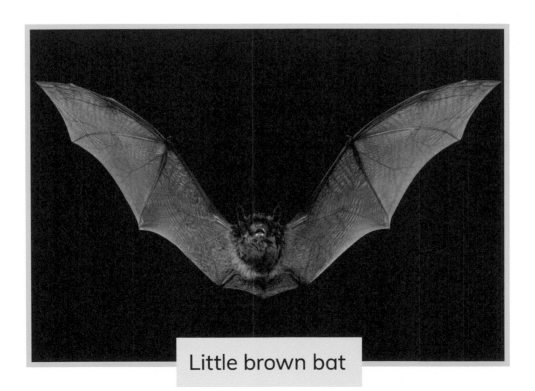

Little brown bat

Fox

Nearby, a fox hunts to feed its babies. The fox **pounces** on a rabbit. It carries the food back to its den.

Late Night

A beaver drags a tree branch to a stream. It is building a **dam**. This will make a pond for the beaver to live in. The beaver works at night to avoid predators.

Beaver

Skunk

A skunk digs for earthworms to eat. Its sense of smell helps it find food in darkness. Skunks eat many types of bugs. They also eat plants and small **mammals**.

Dawn

A red-tailed hawk sits on a high **perch**. It watches for **prey**. A mouse runs across the ground. The hawk swoops down and catches it.

Red-tailed hawk

White-tailed deer

A white-tailed deer walks nearby. The deer nibbles on plants as the sun rises. Another morning in the forest has begun.

Forest Activity

What You Need:

- pencil
- brown construction paper
- scissors
- glue
- blue construction paper
- black construction paper
- green construction paper
- colored pencils, markers, or crayons

What You Do:

1. Trace your hand and part of your arm onto two separate sheets of brown paper.

2. Cut out the tracings. Glue one onto a blue sheet of paper. Glue the other onto a black sheet of paper. These hand shapes are trees.

3. Cut oval shapes from green paper. Glue them on and around the tree branches. These are leaves.

4. Which forest animals come out during the day? Draw three in or near the tree on the blue paper.

5. Which forest animals come out at night? Draw three in or near the tree on the black paper.

6. Glue the backs of the blue and black papers together to make a double-sided forest scene!

Glossary

dam (DAM)—a barrier built across a river or stream to hold back water

echo (EK-oh)—the sound that returns after a traveling sound hits an object

habitat (HAB-uh-tat)—the natural place and conditions in which a plant or animal lives

mammal (MAM-uhl)—a warm-blooded animal that breathes air; mammals have hair or fur; female mammals feed milk to their young

perch (PURCH)—a support on which a bird rests

pounce (POUNSS)—to jump on something suddenly and grab it

predator (PRED-uh-tur)—an animal that hunts other animals for food

prey (PRAY)—an animal hunted by another animal for food

Read More

Duhig, Holly. *Life in the Forest*. New York: Crabtree Publishing Company, 2020.

Gardeski, Christina Mia. *A Year in the Forest*. North Mankato, MN: Capstone, 2020.

Light, Char. *20 Fun Facts about Forest Habitats*. New York: Gareth Stevens Publishing, 2022.

Internet Sites

DK Find Out!—Bats
dkfindout.com/us/animals-and-nature/bats/

National Geographic Kids—Temperate Forest Habitat
kids.nationalgeographic.com/nature/habitats/article/temperate-forest

PBS Kids—A City in the Forest
pbskids.org/plumlanding/educators/context/141_a_city_in_the_forest.html

Index

About the Author

Ellen Labrecque is the author of more than 100 nonfiction children's books. She lives in Bucks County, Pennsylvania, with her husband and two kids. She has the best writing partner in the world—her dog, Oscar. An avid reader and runner, Ellen is a morning person. On most days, she is up before the sun.